Original title:
Plums in the Moonlight

Copyright © 2025 Creative Arts Management OÜ
All rights reserved.

Author: Juliette Kensington
ISBN HARDBACK: 978-1-80586-245-1
ISBN PAPERBACK: 978-1-80586-717-3

Crescent Moon's Embrace

Under a slice of glowing cheese,
The stars munch grapes with ease.
Crickets chirp a midnight tune,
While fireflies dance like quite the loon.

A raccoon swipes a picnic snack,
He wears a mask; that's a fact!
Moonlight giggles in the breeze,
As owls provide the comic tease.

Fragrance of the Night

A scent of mischief fills the air,
With nibbled treats and tales to share.
Mice in capes dart to and fro,
While cats on rooftops steal the show.

The daisies whisper, 'What's the plot?'
One flower's giggling, feeling hot.
As shadows play their silly game,
And nighttime's laughter fuels the fame.

Twilight's Lure

In twilight's grip, the raccoons prance,
With a wobbling, jiggling dance.
The moon's just grinning, having fun,
While frogs perform a flashy run.

A cat sips tea upon the fence,
With clumsy paws, it makes no sense.
'Oh there's the night!' it starts to croon,
As laughter echoes by the moon.

Savoring After Dark

Sweets are stashed beneath the trees,
Where naughty squirrels share a tease.
The sun has slipped, the fun begins,
As shadows chase away their sins.

A feast of chuckles on display,
Starlit mishaps rule the day.
With every giggle, snacks get swiped,
How mischief blooms, and joy is piped.

Evening's Secret Bounty

Underneath the tree where shadows dance,
A purple feast awaits, perchance.
If squirrels could laugh, they'd spill the beans,
On juicy jewels dressed in greens.

The moon peeks down with a cheeky grin,
While critters plot their midnight win.
A feast of sweetness, round and bold,
In nature's grip, so sly and cold.

So gather 'round, you friends of flight,
Let's nibble on the whispers of night.
With every bite, we'll giggle and cheer,
These twilight treasures—we hold so dear.

As night unfolds its puffy shawl,
We'll sing and snack beneath it all.
With every gluttonous smile we share,
The evening's secrets linger in the air.

The Lure of Dusk

As the sun bows low, the stars arrive,
With sticky fingers, we must connive.
Each shadow hides a playful plot,
In darkened corners, magpies trot.

Birds of mischief take to the sky,
Swooping low with a twinkling eye.
Their cackles echo through the cool,
The night has turned into our school.

Oh, to taste the night's fragrant plea,
To nibble on dreams, wild and free.
With giggles sprinkled like stars above,
Whispers of dusk start to shove.

So come along, embrace the night,
For every fruit hides a silly bite.
We'll feast and frolic, never shy,
Under the cloak where secrets lie.

Moonlit Reverie

Beneath the moon, we roam and skip,
With mischief brewing on every lip.
Dancing shadows with eyes agleam,
Under the spell of a playful dream.

The night holds laughter in its hand,
Where giggles spill across the land.
As whispers flutter like tipsy bees,
Our hearts explore with utmost ease.

A stroll through hues of midnight blue,
Hilarity grips both me and you.
With every chuckle, the magic grows,
A charm that only the night bestows.

So take a leap in this moonlit flight,
And gather sweet tales of pure delight.
With each soft chuckle to fill the air,
We unlock the joy that's hidden there.

Velvet Skins of Night

In a velvet coat, the evening flirts,
With glimmering stars and flapping shirts.
These curious fruits, so shiny and bright,
Dare us to pluck 'neath the watchful night.

Complaints from owls drift through trees,
As we munch on dreams with utmost ease.
The laughter spills like a bubbling brook,
Each silly glance is a playful hook.

The night, a canvas of laughter and pranks,
A treasure hunt that the moonlight flanks.
We taste the mischief as giggles arise,
Chasing shadows under starry skies.

So let's indulge in this jolly show,
For the velvet skins of night bestow.
A banquet of laughter just out of sight,
Secretly shared in the laughter of night.

Reflections in the Orchard

Underneath the laughing trees,
Fruit is falling with such ease.
Another snack awaits my hand,
I become a dessert stand!

Raccoons giggle at my plight,
As I munch beneath the light.
Stuck in branches, can't get free,
A snack is worth this mild debris!

Worms politely take their turn,
While I plot my next concern.
Jokes of pits go round and round,
In this sweet chaos, joy is found.

Shadows of Sweetness

The moon winks down on the lane,
As I stalk my fruit campaign.
Cherries laugh, and berries tease,
Catching me, oh such a breeze!

In this orchard, mischief reigns,
Luscious bites hide in the trains.
Nature's candy, how absurd,
Laughing at the birds' own word.

Running off with stolen cheer,
Every squawk is music here.
Whispers of sweetness filled the air,
Leaving me with fruity flair!

Dreams Between the Branches

Caught in dreams of glossy skins,
I approach, where mischief grins.
Hoping for a joyous bite,
Clumsily up, seeking height.

Giggles shake the leafy crowd,
As squirrels dart, oh so proud.
One wrong move, I plummet down,
Landed right beside a clown!

A tumble into sticky fun,
Fruit and laughter now as one.
With every squish, a brand new game,
Who knew fruits could lead to fame?

A Midnight Tasting

Tasting dreams beneath the stars,
Sneaking snacks from neighbors' jars.
Each fruit glimmers as I bide,
Waiting for my chance to slide.

Sipping juice with cheeky grins,
Falling out amid my sins.
As shadows dance and giggles feast,
I find joy in my fruity beast!

Ripe treasures in the dark,
With each bite, I leave my mark.
A comedy of overripe,
Taste this whimsy, take a hike!

Mellowed Nightscapes

Under the sky of velvet hue,
Blushing fruits with dewy view.
Giggles echo through the leaves,
As midnight mischief softly weaves.

Sipping stars from a tiny cup,
Chasing shadows, never give up.
The critters dance, a funny show,
As hiding fruits begin to glow.

Whispers of laughter fill the air,
Each plump delight beyond compare.
A jester moon rolls on its stage,
While playful spirits turn the page.

In a night where chuckles bloom,
Everyone's caught in juicy gloom.
With every bite, a giggle bursts,
In this frolic of whimsical firsts.

Harvesting Moonlight Dreams

In twilight realms where the giggles grow,
Fruit stands rare in a celestial show.
Bouncing shadows leap and play,
Under the watch of a chubby bouquet.

Mischief spills with the harvest cheer,
As critters plot, and puns appear.
A brigade of squirrels, hats askew,
Join in the fun of the nighttime crew.

Under the glow, the laughter flows,
Sippy-straws made from garden hose.
Tiny hands reach for a taste,
While silly giggles fuel their haste.

Chasing the moon with a cheeky grin,
This playful harvest never grows thin.
With each bite of sweetness that they share,
Dreams wrapped in laughter fill the air.

Glorious Shadowed Splendor

In the night where joy is bold,
Round and rosy treats unfold.
Dancing lights with footsteps fleet,
Hidden treasures, oh what a feat!

Beneath the stars, the jokes are ripe,
Squeezed laughter, a zany type.
Giggles tickle the velvet air,
As woodland folk begin to dare.

Shadowed splendor goes hand in hand,
With silliness across the land.
Winking fruits in playful rows,
Invite the whimsy that grows and grows.

With every bite, a story told,
Of laughter rich, hearts never cold.
The sweet night sings its comical tune,
Under the gaze of a savvy moon.

The Allure of Night Harvest

Under the spell of evening's gleam,
The garden blooms, a playful dream.
Midnight fancies waltz and dash,
As gluttons giggle in a silly flash.

Luring creatures from their beds,
For juicy bites and playful threads.
The moon grins wide, a naughty tease,
While laughter rustles through the trees.

With prancing paws and twinkling eyes,
Whimsical antics become the prize.
Chasing the harvest with a spontaneous cheer,
As sweetness reigns—come far and near!

In the cool embrace of night's delight,
Delicious fun takes to flight.
Laughter crops and dreams take shape,
In the allure of this tasty escape.

Ethereal Orchard Tales

In a garden where giggles grow,
Fruits wear hats made of moonlit glow.
A squirrel swings from branch to branch,
Whispering secrets, oh what a chance!

Beneath the stars, the apples dance,
Peaches waltz in a silly prance.
The cherries play tag on the ground,
While shadows chuckle, joy knows no bound.

An elder tree tells jokes severe,
About the pears getting tipsy on beer.
But all the fruit just rolls their eyes,
"C'mon, old friend, we're wise to your lies."

In this orchard of laughter and cheer,
Even the lemons show no fear.
With the moon casting giggles all around,
It's a fruit festival where fun is found!

Kissed by Nightfall

When the sun starts to doze,
The berries wake, in fancy clothes.
With twinkling lights and sparkles bright,
They throw a party all through the night.

The pumpkins jest, dressed in style,
While the grapes join in with a cheeky smile.
They bounce and roll on the grassy floor,
Chasing fireflies, forever wanting more.

Under the watchful moon's wide grin,
Watermelons plot a mischievous win.
They shout, "Let's splatter as we run!
A juicy prank—we'll have our fun!"

With laughter ringing out so clear,
Friends feast on nectar, the night is dear.
In this twilight of humor and glee,
All the fruits celebrate wild and free!

Without Dawn's Gaze

As darkness blankets the sleepy glade,
Giggles bubble where fruits have played.
Strawberries tell tales, wild and spry,
Of the mischievous moon, who winks from the sky.

Peanut butter thoughts dance in the air,
Bananas prank with a golden flair.
Under the stars, jokes fly and spin,
While apples and berries conspire to win.

The night is ripe with laughter's cheer,
As fruits engage in their giddy smear.
Nights without dawn are nights of delight,
When everyone's funny, and nothing feels right.

So, gather round, let's seize the night,
With fruit salad dreams that taste just right.
Under this cover of mischief and fun,
The orchard's alive, and laughter's begun!

Imagining a Fruity Twilight

In a twilight where giggles bloom,
Fruits devise schemes that sparkle and zoom.
A peach rides the breeze with quite a flair,
Waving hello from its golden chair.

Melons whisper secrets in, oh so sweet,
While limes play hopscotch with tiny feet.
"On this breeze of whimsy, let us all soar,
To the land of laughter, where troubles are no more!"

With every chuckle, the sky lights up,
Kiwi juggles lemons from a fanciful cup.
Fruits in the twilight know how to play,
In this magical garden, there's no room for gray.

So as the day fades, come join the spree,
Let's dance with the dragonflies, just you and me.
In this fruity twilight, where fun is the rule,
Every fruit sparkles, it's the party's jewel!

Eclipsed Nectar

In the garden, laughter swells,
Fruits with jokes, oh how they tell.
A pear slips on a laugh so sly,
As apples watch and giggle by.

Moonlit mischief, shadows play,
Bouncing berries, bright and gay.
A raspberry hops, declares a dance,
While cherries laugh, lost in a trance.

Nectar drips from giggling seams,
Caught in whispers, playful dreams.
Bananas slip and swoosh then fall,
Orange jokes, the best of all!

But the best ones hide at night,
Fruits unseen, out of sight.
Dancing in a secret glee,
A fruity farce, wild and free!

Night's Nectarine

Under stars, the nectar shines,
Fruits engage in silly lines.
Grapes fall down, they tumble quick,
Laughing louder, that's their trick.

Peaches poke and tease the pear,
"Do you think I have enough hair?"
The pear just giggles, bound to charm,
While coconuts roll 'round unarm.

A fig tells tales of summer's past,
With every joke, his shadows cast.
Lemons squirt the punchline clear,
While limes all chuckle without fear.

At night, the orchard's wild and bold,
Where laughter ripens, stories unfold.
Like juicy jokes that never spoil,
In moonlit farms, we all recoil!

Sweetness in Shadows

Beneath the moon, a secret scheme,
Where fruits enact a funky dream.
Watermelons giggle wide,
As nectar drips and dreams collide.

Lemons wink with zestful flair,
As berries bounce without a care.
Peas in pods, they burst with cheer,
Ready to croon, with no hint of fear.

In hushed tones, a cantaloupe sings,
Of funny mischief and silly flings.
Tangerines rolling on the green,
With laughter ripe, they're unforeseen.

In shadows, humor finds a home,
Fruity jesters are free to roam.
Under the stars, sweet tales unfurled,
A garden where giggles rule the world!

Breaths of the Orchard

Whispers float through leafy trees,
As cherries chuckle in the breeze.
Oranges claim the title 'King',
While peaches cheer, and do their fling.

Night's embrace brings forth delight,
With apples glinting, ready for flight.
A zesty lime spins tales so bold,
Of furry friends and fruits of gold.

Figgy pranks, a clever jest,
Acting out, they're simply blessed.
Ripe tomatoes join in the game,
With every joke, they share the fame.

In this realm of jovial cheer,
The orchard breathes, the laughs draw near.
With every fruit that takes a stand,
The garden thrives, a merry band!

Fruits of the Ether

In a garden all aglow,
Frantic squirrels put on a show.
Dodging owls as they pick and choose,
It's a fruity feast that they can't lose.

With each nibble, there's a grin,
Why run fast when you can spin?
Under stars that blink and wink,
They laugh at the worries, take a drink.

Chewy bites and soft delights,
Dance around in moonlit nights.
A thump, a hop, a giggle here,
Who knew that snacks would bring such cheer?

Fruits juggled, all in jest,
Flying through the trees, they quest.
Caught at last, they start to wriggle,
What a time, oh what a giggle!

Glistening Secrets

Under the silver glow they gleam,
Fruity whispers, a daring dream.
Bound to splatter with every bite,
It's a juicy, slippery delight!

Bouncing belly laughs surround,
As critters seek the treasure found.
They're bold, ambitious, and quite spry,
Making merry with snacks nearby.

Sipping nectar, sweet and bright,
Crickets sing into the night.
Caught up in a sticky mess,
What a raucous, fun-filled fest!

But watch out for the cheeky thief,
A raccoon slips in, causing grief.
With a wink and a cheeky stare,
He grabs a snack without a care!

Nurtured by Night

Beneath the stars, a friendly scene,
Mischief brews, it's rather keen.
Bouncing hues in nature's glow,
Chasing shadows, high and low.

Sneaky snacks on every branch,
Time for a wild fruit dance!
As laughter spirals through the air,
They'll munch away without a care.

Twirling vines, a scrappy race,
Who will win, the slow or the ace?
A plop! A roll! A giggle burst,
In this moonlit land, they all are cursed!

Sopping faces, sticky hands,
Crafting chaos across the lands.
Glorious madness, pure delight,
In the soft embrace of the night!

Harvest Moon Memoirs

When evening falls, they gather round,
A wildlife party, what a sound.
Chortles and giggles fill the air,
As they reminisce without a care.

Hey there, look at that shiny fruit!
Let's dance and croon—oh, what a hoot!
Raccoons clamber, mice tap-tap,
In this raucous, airborne trap!

Each morsel tells a tale or two,
Friendship found in the midnight dew.
With each bite, a fitting rhyme—
A comedy of endless thyme!

Underneath the harvest glow,
They swap their jokes, high and low.
Late-night antics, fruits on parade,
Together in laughter, memories made!

Radiance in the Gloom

In twilight's embrace, they play hide and seek,
With giggles and laughter, they make us peek.
Round and round, under stars that gleam,
They frolic and tumble, a whimsical dream.

The night air is thick with mischief and cheer,
As shadows dance softly, drawing us near.
With every lost fruit, a chuckle erupts,
While squirrels plan feasts, all guffaws and hiccups.

The Flavor of Shadows

In corners where darkness plays tricks on our eyes,
Mischievous whispers emerge with surprise.
A nibble, a smile, a juicy delight,
Turns frowns into giggles, igniting the night.

Oh, shadows that flicker, do tap dance along,
Each bite is a chorus, a silly sweet song.
Laughter collides with the sweet taste of fun,
While we chase slippery fruits till the rising sun.

Sweet Surrenders

The moon is a jester, pulling pranks from above,
With fruits that entice us, like mischief and love.
Outside, we wander, with dreams in our heads,
Stumbling on laughter, as we follow our threads.

Whispers of sweetness flit among trees,
While giggles escape with the warm summer breeze.
Underneath branches, we gather and grin,
Trading our secrets with each cheeky spin.

Midnight's Temptations

At the stroke of twelve, the silliness grows,
As glimmers of sweetness spring forth from their throes.
With playful pursuits, we tumble and crawl,
Grabbing at treasures, the night's quirky call.

Laughter erupts when we least expect,
As shadows conspire, and chaos collects.
In bites of delight, the world feels anew,
With sprightly jests echoing under the hue.

Secrets of Sunkissed Skin

Underneath the blazing sun,
A picnic turned to laughter won.
Fruits with fuzz, they giggle and tease,
Even the bees join in with ease.

We squished them all, what a delight,
Juicy shenanigans take flight.
Faces sticky, shirts in disarray,
A fruity war, oh what a day!

Lemonade rivers flowing with cheer,
Splashing smiles, that's the frontier.
Fried ants join, they do a jig,
Nature's party, oh so big!

Just as the sun begins to wane,
We snack on fruit, no hint of pain.
Secrets held in skins so bright,
A whole lot of fun in golden light!

Nectar Beyond Twilight

When the stars peek out to play,
We dance and sip the night away.
Bubbles rise like stories told,
Two left feet, but spirits bold.

With nectar sweet, we toast to dreams,
Fruits plump bursting at the seams.
Strawberries wearing capes of green,
At this soirée, we're all too keen.

Laughter echoes in the dark,
A raccoon shows up to leave his mark.
Juggling grapes, he steals the show,
In this night's wild, we go with the flow!

Under twinkling skies, we prank,
While berries dance and slink and crank.
Nectar flowing, all is right,
Funny moments twinkling bright!

Nightfall's Sugary Kiss

As twilight drapes its velvet gown,
We gather 'round with laughter loud.
Sugar kisses float through air,
Witty tales beyond compare.

Bananas sport their sunny grins,
Mischief brews amid the spins.
Marshmallow clouds and berry bombs,
Tickled toes and cheeky charms.

Pineapple hats and berry bows,
We're all aglow, forget our woes.
With every bite, we giggle some,
In this fruity fun, we've just begun!

Jam-sticky fingers weave their tale,
We ride the laughter like a sail.
Nightfall's kiss brings us delight,
Our joyful feast steals the night!

The Lure of Galaxy Fruits

In a garden of colors bright,
Fructal wonders, pure delight.
Galactic fruits with silly names,
They plop and float like playful games.

Starfruits twinkle, dreams take flight,
As we gobble under moonlight.
Banana comets zoom through space,
Every bite a wild embrace.

The cosmos' charm, sweet and weird,
Laughter bubbles, nothing feared.
Alien berries wear a grin,
As we twirl and dance within!

Giggling grapes roll off the rocks,
Comets nibble, they'll steal the box.
Under starlit skies, we unite,
Fruity fun ignites the night!

Cradled in the Night

In the dark, with laughter loud,
A bunch of fruits, oh what a crowd!
They giggle and wiggle, such a sight,
Dance in the shadows, oh what delight!

Round and round, they do a jig,
Crisp skin glowing, oh so big!
Under stars, they spin and sway,
Who knew fruit could dance this way?

Whispering Fruits

Beneath the stars, they share their dreams,
Sweet-tart secrets, like playful beams.
One cheeky berry shouts with glee,
"No fridge for us, we're wild and free!"

In the hush, they trade their tales,
Of cheeky birds and wind-swept gales.
They burst with laughter, oh what fun!
Even the crickets wait for a pun.

Moonbeams on Ripe Flesh

A shiny orb above their heads,
Casting light where laughter spreads.
Juicy jokes and pokes abound,
In this silly night, joy is found!

With giggles bouncing off the air,
Fruit friends tease without a care.
"Who's juicier, I'm juicy too!"
It's a fruity contest, oh who knew?

Enchanted Harvest

In the field, a merry cheer,
As fruits unite, no hint of fear.
With every laugh, they make a mess,
What a sight, this fruit-filled fest!

Harvest moon, round and bright,
Inviting jokes throughout the night.
Shiny skins and winked eyes,
Under the stars, the fun supplies!

Sliced Stars

The stars up high are cut like pie,
I'd grab a fork and eat 'em spry.
Each twinkle's just a shiny slice,
And if they fall, I'll take a bite!

A galaxy with flavors bright,
Licorice black and candy white.
I snack on dreams and cosmic rays,
While giggling at their silly ways.

The comets trail like frosting sweet,
A confection made for us to meet.
And in this feast of stellar cheer,
I toast to snacks both far and near!

So let the night bring tasty lore,
Of nibbled wishes and much more.
With every crunch, the jokes will fly,
As we munch stars beneath the sky!

Fruitful Nightfall

When evening drops its fruity cloak,
I chuckle at the silly oak.
It winks at me, seems quite bemused,
By jokes my silly mind has bruised.

The berries blush in dusky light,
As laughter bounces, pure delight.
Each giggle bursts like bubbling juice,
A sunny splash of wild excuse!

A bunch of grapes falls off the vine,
They tumble down, a merry line.
With every squish, a joke appears,
A fruity punchline spreads the cheers!

So here we dance with vines entwined,
While sweetened air laughs, unconfined.
Beneath the moon, we feast and play,
In fruit-filled frolics, night and day!

Aromas Beneath the Moon

The night is ripe with scents so bold,
Like secret tales yet to be told.
I sniff the air and giggle bright,
A whiff of pie, the moon's delight!

A waft of honey tickles my nose,
The jasmine whispers sweetly, who knows?
I dance through fragrances that tease,
With funny fables floating in the breeze.

The oranges roll with laughter loud,
While lemons pout beneath the cloud.
I squeeze them tight to hear them squeak,
Their citrus jokes are never bleak!

So join me in this scented chase,
Where laughter blooms and dreams embrace.
As moonlit aromas spin around,
We'll giggle till the sun is found!

A Dance of Nightshade

In gardens lush, where shadows play,
The nightshade grins, in a cheeky way.
It twirls so sly with sly surprise,
With winks and waves from leafy eyes.

The tomatoes giggle, ripe and red,
While radishes hide and hardly tread.
"Oh, what a night!" the broccoli sings,
As veggies jive on veggies' swings!

The moonlight casts a silly trick,
A dance-off spurs, oh, what a kick!
Eggplants laugh, they take the floor,
In veggie jests, we crave for more!

So come and join this leafy spree,
With roots that dance so carefree.
In shadows rich, the laughter plants,
A nightshade dance that always enchants!

Harvesting Dreams

Beneath the stars, we reach for skies,
With bags in hand and twinkling eyes.
A ladder's leaning, oh so tall,
As giggles echo with each small fall.

The fruit we chase is sweet and round,
Yet sticky hands are all we've found.
We pluck and juggle, what a sight!
With midnight snacks, we feast tonight.

A raccoon joins with sly delight,
Claiming treasures in the twilight.
We laugh and scurry, what a race,
As he outsmarts us with his grace.

So gather 'round and raise a cheer,
For dreams are fruit, let's make it clear.
In night's embrace, we'll share the jest,
For laughter ripens, and we're blessed.

Nightfall's Abundance

The garden glows with moonlit cheer,
Where odd-shaped shadows dance near.
A creature lurks with hopes so high,
Expecting sweets as we pass by.

We sneak around, with stealthy flair,
But branches crack, oh, what a scare!
The fruit we harvest seems so bold,
Yet slips away with laughter told.

A cat leaps high, joins in the fun,
As startled crickets start their run.
All gathered here, the mischief calls,
We'll fill our hands, ignore the falls.

So while the night spins tales so grand,
We munch on dreams and band together,
With every bite, our spirits rise,
For joy is best when shared and wise.

The Dance of Night Fruits

Under the moon, we start to sway,
As fruits above decide to play.
They roll and tumble, oh what a spree,
Each one a dancer, wild and free.

The branches bend with giggles bright,
As shadows twirl in the soft moonlight.
One slips and lands upon our head,
A fruity crown from dreams we've fed.

Laughter bubbles, with laughter's tune,
As we share bites beneath the moon.
Each one we taste, it's such delight,
These nocturnal performers shine so bright.

So let us cheer, for whims galore,
Each bite a smile, a sweet encore.
We'll dance and laugh till dawn's first glow,
As night fruits whirl in joyous flow.

Dew-kissed Serenades

With morning leaves all glistening bright,
We tiptoe out for a fruity bite.
Dew drops dangle like jewels rare,
As we embark on our sweet affair.

A squirrel scurries, with furry flair,
He joins our quest, now we're a pair.
We giggle softly, plotting schemes,
While dreaming loud of fruity dreams.

Our baskets fill, but so do our cheeks,
As we snack between our playful squeaks.
Nature's bounty, oh, what a treat,
Each nibble's a dance, oh so sweet!

So here's to nights and mornings too,
Where laughter bubbles, fresh as dew.
With every bite, we sing and play,
In this fruity world, we'll lose our way.

Luminous Ripeness

Under the glow of the cheeky night,
Fruits chuckle in their juicy delight.
Squirrels dance with a silly flair,
Whispering secrets without a care.

Moonbeam giggles tickle the trees,
As shadows play tag with the breeze.
Laughter burst from a high branch,
While rabbits join in a merry dance.

A funny frog croaks a tune so bright,
He's a star in this fruity sight.
With beetles applauding his show,
They wiggle and jiggle in a fun-flow.

In this garden, where silliness reigns,
Each fruit wears a crown, no refrains.
Tonight, they toast to the lunar glow,
With winks and wobbles, they let it flow.

Evening's Taste

In twilight's embrace, where giggles swell,
A fruit party starts, can you tell?
Grapes tell jokes, while cherries grin,
Sneaky peaches plotting a twin.

A cheeky breeze sways each vine,
And lemons twist, saying, 'Aren't we fine?'
Laughter bubbles like fizzy drink,
While apples nod, winking, 'Don't you think?'

Under the stars, a weird fruit crew,
Throwing a bash, just for a few.
Loony lemons fall into a pie,
While berries bounce and say, 'Oh my!'

At evening's taste, they raise a cheer,
With nutty humor, "When's dessert, dear?"
In this wild feast, the night's just right,
As fruits take the stage in pure delight.

The Fruit of Starlight

In a cosmic dance, they swirl with glee,
Fruits in orbit, all wild and free.
Mangoes crack jokes, kiwi makes faces,
While berries roll through outer spaces.

Raspberry giggles echo the night,
Changing the stars with its berry might.
Bananas peel laughter, slipping high,
As cosmic fruits all laugh and sigh.

Jokes bounce off comets, a fruity delight,
Strawberries plan a wild moonlit flight.
With twinkling eyes, they shimmer and glow,
A wacky gala only fruits know.

Floating in starlight, they shake their heads,
Laughing at dreams and whimsical spreads.
In this fruit circus, all is a game,
In the glow of laughter, never the same.

Radiance in the Dark

When shadows stretch, and silliness wakes,
Fruits gather 'round for the chuckle it makes.
Peaches giggle, as plump pears boast,
Gathering laughter, their favorite host.

Squashed in the shadows, they plot a prank,
Nuts bounce around, feeling quite frank.
A playful melon swings from the vine,
Saying, 'Hey buddies, let's all dine!'

With radiant smiles in the thick of night,
Fruits jive and shimmer, oh what a sight.
They toast to the laughter that comes with the dark,
Stir up some mischief with each little spark.

In this radiance where humor's a must,
Every fruit sparkles, in laughter, they trust.
Who knew the night could be such a show?
With each silly moment, they let it flow.

Serene Harvests

Beneath the stars, fruits lie in wait,
A raccoon's feast, oh, what a fate!
With sticky paws and sneaky grace,
He dances through the mystic space.

Giggling at shadows that hop and sway,
The moon grins big and bright today.
A jubilee of taste and tease,
With every bite, a nibble's breeze.

Laughter whispers through the trees,
As crickets chirp their nighttime tease.
What's that jingle? Oh, it's just me,
A plump fruit rolling joyfully!

So raise a toast to the midnight crew,
With fruits divine, and skies so blue.
Let's dance and prance without a care,
In this harvest, we all will share!

Embracing the Fruitful Night

When twilight drapes its velvet cloak,
And trees begin to giggle and poke.
Glorious orbs swaying up high,
I swear I saw one wink and fly!

A feast awaits, oh what a thrill,
Sipping juice from a garden chill.
In the moonlight's playful reach,
An orchard hosts a silly speech.

Bumbling bees join in the cheer,
Buzzing secrets, oh dear, oh dear!
A fruit parade in the midnight air,
How can we not laugh and share?

A chubby squirrel with a cheeky grin,
Joins the fun with a spin and spin.
In this bizarre, delightful plight,
We dance with joy through the fruitful night!

Night's Silken Offerings

The night unfolds with plush delights,
As fuzzy globes start their antics, right?
A murmur of laughter floats around,
With each sweet bite of joy unbound.

A fox in a hat, what a silly sight,
Swiping treats under the moonlight.
The bushes giggle, the branches sway,
Joyful chaos rules the play today.

Juicy treasures tumble and roll,
Crispy leaves dance, oh what a stroll!
Watch as critters trade and tease,
In this harvest, we aim to please.

With every nibble and every cheer,
The quirkiest night of the whole year.
Laughter echoes 'neath the stars,
The moon reflects our fruity wars!

Cerulean Bliss

Under the blue, the mischief brews,
Knocking on heavens, what do we choose?
With every round, our giggles grow,
A stash of fun, on with the show!

The owls blink back with clever glee,
As what's this? A dance-off at three!
Claiming the harvest with step and twirl,
As fruity favors cause hearts to whirl.

Chasing shadows, oh what a spree,
An orange rolls fast, but can't escape me!
Laughter wraps 'round like a cozy quilt,
In this blissful night, spirits are built.

So here we toast to the fruits that greet,
With a wink and a giggle, tonight's so sweet.
May the gelato of joy always stay,
In our hearts where the silliness plays!

Fruits of the Night Sky

In the garden where shadows creep,
Fruits giggle as they softly sleep.
Stars sprinkle whispers from on high,
While crickets croon a lullaby.

A banana slips, oh what a sight!
It dreams of slipping through the night.
Berries roll with a jolly cheer,
As moonbeams join the fruit parade here.

The apples clink, toasts all around,
A fruity party, joy unbound.
In this orchard where laughter thrives,
Each bite brings forth zany high-fives.

With every laugh, the night grows bold,
As berries boast about their gold.
A cherry winks, it's all in fun,
In this moonlit frolic, we've just begun.

Luminous Harvest

Under the glow of the moon's soft gaze,
Fruits gossip wildly in delightful ways.
A sassy kiwi, with a wink and nod,
Declares, "I'm the star, I'm the fruiting god!"

A peach with flair, begins to shimmy,
While grapes groove along, feeling all zippy.
Bananas swing and twirl with glee,
They're the main act in this fruity spree.

The pears crack jokes that tickle the vine,
As shadows dance, everything's just fine.
Citrus slices chime a laughter hymn,
In the orchard, lights are never dim.

In this cabaret, what a delight,
As fruits unite under the starry night.
With every chuckle, the harvest grows,
One ripe giggle after another flows.

Shadows of Sweetness

When the sun dips low, the mischief awakes,
The fruits plan pranks and giggling shakes.
A cantaloupe wears a silly hat,
While lemons plot a zesty spat.

Beyond the hedge, a grape hangs low,
Whispering secrets that only they know.
Raspberry raves, "Let's have a ball!"
As cherries join in, they giggle and fall.

Under the stars, the cantaloupe spins,
While a trio of figs do silly twin grins.
Quips of the night float soft and sweet,
In this jocular grove, oh what a feat!

The laughter twinkles like stars above,
In this evening crush, there's endless love.
With every pun and fruity jest,
The garden thrives, and we're truly blessed.

Celestial Orchard

In a realm where the silly fruits grow,
They throw a bash with a celestial glow.
A dancing pineapple leads the crew,
While the elderberry plays peek-a-boo.

Orchard tales fly like fireflies bright,
Each one a giggle, a whimsical sight.
The watermelon floats, a dreamy delight,
In this zany orchard of pure moonlight.

Cherries whistle songs from days gone past,
As fig and plum have a fun-filled blast.
Apricots cheer, their golden hue,
In this cosmic party, they're all such a brew!

With every high-five, they swing and sway,
Under the stars, they laugh and play.
A slice of moon hides behind a cloud,
As this fruity laughter gathers a crowd.

Illuminated Edibles

Under a glow of silvery cheer,
The fruits wink with mischief near.
A nibble here, a giggle there,
In twilight's dance, we lose our care.

Silly shapes on branches sway,
Tickled leaves in night's ballet.
A cheeky bite, oh what delight!
Laughter blooms in starry sight.

Render the harvest, pile them high,
Magic whispers in the sky.
With every splash of juice that drips,
We laugh and dance, exchange our quips.

A moonlit feast on nature's plate,
Forks and jokes at every rate.
Let's savor each odd flavor found,
In this night's garden all around.

Embrace of the Night

In shadows deep, where giggles share,
Fruits wear grins, a playful flare.
Plucked with care from the night's embrace,
Laughter echoes in this space.

Each bite's a joke, a riddle sweet,
Round and juicy, a silly treat.
They bounce around in rhythmic flare,
A game we play without a care.

A cheeky twist, the stars align,
Juicy surprises that intertwine.
Moonlit whispers tease our taste,
Each nibble met with joyful haste.

Under the moon's shimmering haze,
We feast and giggle, lost in praise.
These fruity treasures make us bright,
In the embrace of another night.

Celestial Fruits of the Evening

Stars plucked from the cosmic tree,
Fall as laughter, wild and free.
Each twinkle hides a fruity jest,
In this moonlit, merry fest.

Flavor bursts, a shocking glee,
The sweetest laughs spill endlessly.
Comets dance, a wild parade,
In the orchard, serenades.

A cosmic joke, a sight so rare,
Bouncing fruits float through the air.
They giggle softly, ripe and round,
In every corner, joy is found.

Nibble slowly, don't be shy,
Join the feast beneath the sky.
A playful night, let's toast and cheer,
To fruity quirks we all hold dear.

Night's Verdant Secrets

Under the cloak of dark delight,
Kooky treasures spark the night.
Whispers of flavors hide and seek,
In every burst, a giggle speaks.

Leaves snicker at what we chase,
Juicy secrets in this place.
With every nibble, laughter flows,
In moonlit games, the mischief grows.

Dare to taste the wild unknown,
In this garden, we're not alone.
Tonight our taste buds come alive,
Through silly bites, we thrive and jive.

Let's crunch and munch till dawn's soft glow,
Sharing smiles as the good vibes flow.
In these verdant shadows, we unite,
Savoring joys of the playful night.

Under the Silver Sky

Beneath the shimmer, laughter springs,
A raccoon dances, twirls, and sings.
With berry hats and jam-stained paws,
He throws a party without a cause.

The stars are guests, they wink and sway,
While fireflies zap around in play.
A hedgehog juggles acorn pies,
While owls hoot out some silly cries.

Twilight Soliloquy

In the dark, a gopher frets,
His dinner plans are full of bets.
With carrot cake and grape juice bold,
He's hoping for the best to unfold.

A bat arrives, quite out of breath,
With tales of snacks and near-Death.
They share a laugh, a silly tale,
As shadows dance, like cheese and quail.

Lush Nocturne

A squirrel plays the flute with flair,
While crickets groove without a care.
The mushrooms nod, they start to sway,
Inviting all to join the play.

The moon spills milk on grassy floors,
As rascally frogs burst through the doors.
With spoons in paws, they slurp and grin,
Creating mischief that won't wear thin.

Midnight's Palette

A badger sprinkles glitter bright,
On marshmallow clouds that float at night.
The colors blend, a fruity whirl,
As cheeky rabbits dance and twirl.

Balloons of jelly bounce so high,
While cats in capes zoom 'cross the sky.
With laughter loud, the stars align,
In this sweet chaos, all is fine.

Night's Gentle Bounty

Under the stars, a feast awaits,
Fruit so sweet, it tempts our fates.
We giggle softly, a playful tease,
Gathering treasures with utmost ease.

A raccoon watches, its eyes all aglow,
Planning a raid with a sly little show.
We shoo him away with a laugh and a cheer,
Only to stumble on our fruit-filled sphere.

But who would have thought, in the moon's bright light,
That fruit could inspire such joyous plight?
We dance round the tree, dodging branches so low,
While nature's mischief puts on a show.

In the end, we're left with our harvest so fine,
With cheeky smiles and our spirits entwined.
Eating our bounty, no cares left to pluck,
In the laughter of night, we've all struck good luck.

Silken Shadows

As shadows stretch, they tease and sway,
We tiptoe softly, ready to play.
A soft breeze whispers, 'Come take a bite,'
In the garden of dreams, everything's bright.

A squirrel darts, wearing a cap of leaves,
Pulling pranks that nobody believes.
We chase him around with giggles ablaze,
Lost in a whirlwind of sticky sun rays.

The green fruits smile with a mischievous grin,
Promising chaos, we know we'll give in.
Plump and inviting, they beckon us near,
While we plot our next giggle-filled cheer.

In silken shadows, mischief unfolds,
Each taste a laughter, a story retold.
The night is alive with a spark and a dance,
In the world of our whims, all souls take a chance.

The Temptation of Twilight

When twilight falls, giggles arise,
In the secret garden, bright, surprise!
We sneak and whisper, our hearts on fire,
Every rustle ignites playful desire.

The fruit-hued treasures wink back at us,
We gather round, creating a fuss.
A sprinkle of daring, a dash of delight,
Spurred by the glow of the coming night.

Fingers sticky, smiles wide as can be,
Mischief brewed in this fruity spree.
With crumbs in our hair and juice on our chin,
In the world of twilight, we celebrate sin.

The moon peeks down, a cheeky moonbeam,
As laughter and joy weave through our dream.
With each little bite, our antics soar high,
In twilight's embrace, we let out a sigh.

Hoarded Fragrance

In corners hidden, aromas abound,
A secret stash where treasures are found.
We giggle and plot with mischievous grins,
For laughter ignites as the frugal begins.

The sweetness rumbles, a symphonic smell,
With every sniff, we're under its spell.
Our stash of the night, the bounty we claim,
Hoarded giggles, we're wild in this game.

Each fragrant plunder is a moment worth glee,
We dance in the moonlight, both wild and free.
As we munch on our winnings, our spirits collide,
In the hoard of the night, our joy cannot hide.

With empty bowls, we collapse with delight,
The laughter drifts softly, the stars shining bright.
In the end, it's clear, with no cause to gloom,
We've turned a simple night into a room full of bloom.

Moonlit Gatherings

Under the glow of a silver beam,
Fruits dance wildly, a funny dream.
Bright faces giggle in shadowed light,
As we munch on goodies, what a sight!

The branches creak as laughter flows,
Who knew fruit could bring such woes?
Silly slips and fumbled grabs,
It's a fruit-fest, and we're the jabs!

With each bite, a juicy surprise,
Sticky fingers, oh how we pry!
The moon winks down at our fun spree,
In this orchard, though, there's no decree!

So raise a toast to this night so bright,
Where laughter sparkles, a pure delight.
In the shadowy orchard, we celebrate,
In moonlit gatherings, we simply create!

Celestial Bounty

Stars twinkle down on our food crusade,
Snatching snacks before they fade.
We've got silly faces after each bite,
Who knew strawberries could take flight?

The celestial bounty, oh what a sight,
Every taste leads to a new delight.
With gummy worms and fruit-filled pies,
The stars above chuckle, oh what a prize!

We toss around the leftover pips,
Hilarity ensues with every trip.
Squinting at shadows, we try to spot,
The fruit pirates that we forgot!

So gather 'round, our merry crew,
Under this cosmic canopy so blue.
In this funny feast, we revel and sing,
For in every laugh, we find the spring!

Nocturnal Delights

The moon calls out, a giggling chat,
Found some fruit, imagine that!
Like little critters, we scurry about,
Nibbling and munching with shouts of doubt.

Sweet treasures hide beneath leaves lush,
With each discovery comes a blush.
Who tossed this berry? It's quite a mess,
We all agree, it's anyone's guess!

Beneath the stars we share our snacks,
With juicy jokes to fill the cracks.
Silly dances and laughter loud,
Nocturnal delights make us proud!

So gather your friends, don't miss the boat,
Find a good apple, and take a note.
In the night's embrace, fun takes flight,
Our harvest of laughter, pure delight!

Secrets of the Night Orchard

In shadows deep, a secret place,
Where fruit whispers with a silly grace.
With giggles shared, we plot and plan,
In this orchard, we're the fan!

What's this? A hidden stash over here?
A rogue banana, lurking near.
As giggles escape with every peel,
Our secret laughs turn into a deal.

Each taste reveals a funny tale,
Of fruit and friends, we never fail.
With every bite, we're on a quest,
To discover flavors that are the best!

So tiptoe soft, keep your eyes wide,
In this night orchard, let joy abide.
For secrets sweet and laughter bold,
Are treasures that never get old!

Midnight Nectar

Sneaky bites beneath the stars,
Fruit drips down like ruined cars.
Laughter echoes through the night,
A sticky dance, what a sight!

Sumptuous jewels on the tree,
Sipping juice, just you and me.
Chasing shadows, giggles swell,
Underneath the leafy spell.

Ripe desires in the moon's embrace,
Wobbly steps, a silly chase.
Comets wink, we steal a few,
With every bite, we snicker, too!

Crispy skies, a crunch so bold,
Stories of the night retold.
Sticky fingers, giddy grins,
This summer's fun, it truly wins!

Silvery Boughs

Branches bend with gleeful weight,
Mischief lingers, isn't fate?
Nibbles shared in whispered tones,
Cheeky smiles and silly groans.

Glorious fruit, a fragrant tease,
Charmed by rustling in the breeze.
We weave tales as we munch,
Tasting joy with every crunch.

Hilarity hides in every peel,
A burst of laughter, oh what a meal!
Twinkling lights above us shine,
With each bite, the world is fine!

Falling leaves, a starlit show,
Silly antics, one to grow.
Underneath the shimmering sky,
Delightful moments, oh my, oh my!

Twilight's Juicy Secrets

Whispers float with fragrant lies,
Tasting secrets in the skies.
Nibbles shared with grinning glee,
Beams of laughter, just you and me.

Slippery skins, oh such a tease,
Juicy smirks carried on the breeze.
On this night, let worries fade,
As juicy treasures are displayed.

Mischief springs from every bite,
A giggly dash in fading light.
Splashes of colors, sweet delight,
With every taste, the world feels right.

Luminous laughter, a merry crew,
Chasing flavors, just me and you.
Beneath the stars, we share a cheer,
In this twilight, mischief is near!

Dreamy Dusk Delights

A dancing glow in evening's whim,
Ripe reflections on each limb.
Echoes of giggles fill the air,
With every bite, we're almost bare.

Juicy madness, let's not pause,
In this moment, we're the cause.
Moonlit ruckus, tastes divine,
With sticky fingers, hearts align.

Tickled toes on grassy beds,
Mouths agape and spinning heads.
A symphony of crunch and slurp,
In this frenzy, no one's a cur!

Twilight tales, a whimsical find,
With playful hearts, we leave behind.
Under starlight's twinkling charm,
These dreamy dusk delights disarm!

Charmed by the Stars

Under the sky, a fruity delight,
A dance with the shadows, all through the night.
Bright laughs echo from trees up so high,
As giggles and snacks chase the moon on the sky.

With dreams of sweet bites in a silly parade,
Who knew those fat fruits could bring such charade?
The moon peeks down, a grin on her face,
As we munch and we munch—oh, what a fine place!

What mischief awaits, just around the bend?
A race to the orchard, let's see who can blend!
With fruits in our pockets, we'll clamber and climb,
Laughing aloud, oh, how sublime!

So here's to the night, with its laughter and glee,
With bites so divine, we're as happy as can be.
Beneath the twinkling, oh what a surprise,
We'll feast 'til the morning, with stars in our eyes.

Nocturnal Flavor

In the dark, a taste like never before,
Sweetness erupts—let's see who can score!
Under the stars, on a quest for a snack,
With giggles and tumbles, we're never looking back.

A crunch and a munch in this midnight delight,
Slips and falls add to our laughter tonight.
In search of the juice that's hidden away,
We squabble and tumble, it's a wild, fruity fray!

Who knew that the night held such flavorful fun?
With each silly spill, there's joy on the run.
The stars are our audience, the moon is our cheer,
As we feast on the fruits, with no hint of fear!

So gather your friends for a night full of cheer,
With flavors that burst—oh, the laughter is near!
Let's make this a night we'll never forget,
With flavors and fun, oh, we're not done yet!

Starlit Indulgence

Under the cosmos, sweet cravings arise,
Laughter and mischief, igniting the skies.
Chasing the flavors, like kids on the run,
With sprinkled delights, oh, this night, what fun!

Fruits tumble like stars, all over the ground,
We giggle and wiggle, with joy all around.
A mishap occurs—a fruit flies away,
But laughter ignites as we wish it would stay!

With each bite we savor, oh, what a surprise,
The moon nudges gently, with laughter in her eyes.
Let's gather these moments, sweet treasures in hand,
Dancing in shadows, like grains of fine sand.

So raise up your glasses to midnight's sweet treat,
To laughter and joy, we'll never concede!
With stars as our blanket and joy in the air,
We'll feast on our dreams, with memories to share.

Whispering Garden

In a garden at night, where secrets abound,
Tangled in giggles, our laughter resounds.
Beneath the bright moon, full of whimsy and cheer,
With whispers of sweetness, alive and so near.

Around every corner, a curious bite,
Fruit mischief calls us, oh, what a sight!
We slip and we slide, in this fruity domain,
Sneaks and surprise as we dance through the lane.

A night filled with glee, let's eat 'til we're full,
With cheers and with antics, life's bright and never dull.
Each laughter we share is a flavor that's spun,
In this magical garden, oh, how we have fun!

So here's to the evenings of whispering fate,
With snacks and sweet joy, let's elegantly sate!
In the glow of soft night, where memories play,
We'll feast on our delights, come join in the fray!

Gleaming Fruit Echoes

In the garden where giggles grow,
Fruits are dancing in a moonlit show.
Chasing shadows that tease and play,
Join the party where mischief sways.

Bouncing berries sing out loud,
As squirrels sneak in, feeling proud.
A splash of juice sends a grin,
While fireflies join the fruity din.

Pick a pear, give it a shake,
Watch it roll, what a silly mistake!
Laughter lingers in the night,
As fruit flies twirl in delight.

With each bite, the jokes are sweet,
In this orchard, no one can cheat.
So grab a snack, take a seat,
Life's a feast, oh what a treat!

Night's Silken Gifts

Under the stars, the gifts arrive,
In a spool of threads, the fruits all thrive.
Laughter floats on a gentle breeze,
Whispers of fun among the trees.

A cheeky peach plays peek-a-boo,
A giggling apple shimmies too.
Bananas dance as if in a trance,
While berries wiggle, joining the dance.

With each pluck, a chuckle bursts,
As playful fruit quench our thirsts.
Night's banquet spreads, a comical sight,
Where everyone's nibbling with sheer delight.

So let the critters join in the fray,
As we munch on joy till the break of day.
Under the sky, so vast and bright,
Chomping away in the dim twilight!

Under Lunar Glow

In the glow of the silvery round,
Fruits of laughter swirl all around.
A mishap here, a tumble there,
Joyful chaos fills the air.

A merry grape rolls off its path,
Bouncing along, invoking a laugh.
Cherries giggle, their cheeks so round,
Spinning tales of silliness found.

Mangoes strut with outrageous flair,
As oranges tumble without a care.
Under the stars, the party's bold,
Where every bite brings joy to unfold.

With each munch, the fun does grow,
A banquet of smiles, stealing the show.
In this fruit-filled, whimsical row,
We'll dance till dawn, in the lunar glow!

Shadows of Midnight Harvest

In the night where shadows creep,
Fruits are plotting their secret sweep.
Underneath the sleepy skies,
Berries giggle with wide-open eyes.

A rogue fig sneaks a daring bite,
While the lemons toss in pure delight.
They roll and tumble in playful strife,
Creating laughter, full of life.

With each harvest, a prank unfolds,
A watermelon's tale finally told.
As all the flavors collide and blend,
The joy of the crop has no end.

So let them frolic, let them play,
These midnight stars, come join the fray.
In shadows cast, the giggles weave,
A banquet of fun; who wouldn't believe?

Juices of Dusk

In the garden, a fruit takes flight,
A plump little rogue, what a sight!
Dancing with stars, they wiggle and sway,
Chasing the fireflies that come out to play.

Laughter erupts as a cat gives chase,
To the swirling shadows in this fruity space.
With splashes of color, they tumble and roll,
Making a mess that's part of the goal.

Fruits giggle softly, their skins shiny bright,
Joking with crickets that sing through the night.
"Try to catch us, you silly old man!"
They tease from the branches, a mischievous plan.

But be careful, dear friends, when you take a treat,
For the juice might just land on your shoes or your feet.
With a splat and a splash that creates quite the scene,
You might find you're now part of their team!

Orchard Whispers

In the orchard where giggles grow,
Fruits chat softly, stealing the show.
"Can you hear that? It's a rumor divine,
The apples are plotting; they think they're just fine!"

The cherries chuckle, with a wink and a twirl,
"Those apples are fools, let them unfurl!"
Each branch has secrets, with whispers of glee,
As the moonlight wraps round, like a warm, cozy tee.

Squirrels leap high, with mischief in mind,
Stealing the berries, leaving none behind.
A raucous retreat, they chatter and dash,
With a laughter so bright, it's a playful clash.

But the neighboring pears, with their dignified stance,
Join the fun, unaware of their chance.
"Lend us your ears!" the grapes shout with cheer,
For in this wild evening, there's nothing to fear!

Silvery Night Fruits

Under the glow of a silvery sphere,
Fruits come alive, and we gather near.
"Who can do the best fruit dance?" they call,
With big round bulges, they bounce and they sprawl.

Watermelons wobble, while cherries can flip,
With lemons so sour, they pucker and slip.
It's a circus of flavors, a berrylicious jam,
As we all try to join in with a slam!

Bananas get dizzy, while peaches just pout,
"Let's make it a challenge, we'll show them what's stout!"
But overconfident apples come tumbling down,
As the laughter erupts, they just wear a frown.

Yet the night doesn't end as the songbirds ring,
With fruity-high dreams, we just want to sing.
For in the enchanted light, we all have our quirks,
Who knew such delights could come from our works?

Twilight's Sweet Offering

Twilight spills laughter from branches so wide,
Fruits joke with the breeze, like friends side by side.
"Who brought the honey? Who poured out the cheer?"
Cries a fig, rolling in giggles, oh dear!

In the backyard show, each fruit takes its turn,
To share their sweet tales that make our hearts yearn.
"Listen closely!" a plucky peach claims,
"I once wore a crown for my juicy good games!"

Mulberries croon in a velvety tune,
While the starfruit sparkles like the stars in June.
"Let's throw a big bash!" shouts a whimsied lime,
"We'll dance till the dawn, it'll be just sublime!"

So twilight's sweet offering brings smiles anew,
As we laugh with the fruits and enjoy each view.
In the magical dusk with skies fading bright,
Together we revel, in pure, fruity light!

www.ingramcontent.com/pod-product-compliance
Lightning Source LLC
Chambersburg PA
CBHW062108280426
43661CB00086B/342